LES PETITS PLATS
FRANÇAIS
SIMON & SCHUSTER
ILLUSTRATED

irresistible macaroons

JOSÉ MARÉCHAL

Photography by Akiko Ida
Styling by Sonia Lucano

SIMON &
SCHUSTER

London · New York · Sydney · Toronto

A CBS COMPANY

English language edition published in Great Britain by
Simon and Schuster UK Ltd, 2010
A CBS Company

SIMON AND SCHUSTER ILLUSTRATED BOOKS
Simon & Schuster UK
222 Gray's Inn Road
London WC1X 8HB
www.simonandschuster.co.uk

2 3 4 5 6 7 8 9 10

Styling for photography: Sonia Lucano

Translation: Prudence Ivey
Copy editor English language: Nicki Lampon

Colour reproduction by Dot Gradations Ltd, UK
Printed and bound in U.A.E.

ISBN 978-0-85720-109-6

Contents

Equipment

Oven
The make of your oven doesn't matter, although fan-assisted ovens will cook more evenly. What is important is mastering your oven and cooking utensils, so do not hesitate to adapt the temperature by a few degrees or the cooking time by a few minutes to suit your oven.

Scales
Precision is essential when making macaroons. Don't think 'close enough' when it comes to proportions. A few grams more or less can cause considerable variation in the consistency of the meringue and the appearance of your macaroons.
Note: 1 egg white weighs approximately 30 g (1 oz).

Sieve
This is essential to refine the mix of icing sugar and ground almonds and prevent lumps of powder making ugly bumps in the surface of your macaroons.

Thermometer
To measure the temperature of the sugar syrup, use a sugar thermometer that measures up to 200°C (400°F). Electric thermometers are handy as they are extremely precise, although they are more expensive.

Electric whisk or food processor
A food processor allows you to keep your hands free to do other things (such as choose the shade of colouring) while waiting for the egg whites to stiffen. If you have a hand-held electric whisk, beat the eggs using regular, circular motions. They will rise better and more quickly.

Spatula
This utensil is indispensable for making macaroons, especially when incorporating the meringue with the almond paste; without a spatula, the egg white would collapse too much. Plastic or silicone spatulas are more supple than wood or metal and so allow greater precision.

Piping bag with a nozzle of 8–10 mm (⅜–½ inch)
For mini macaroons of 3 cm (1¼ inches) diameter, you can use either nozzle while figuring out the correct amount of paste to pipe. A piping bag makes obtaining a regular, pretty, round macaroon much easier. You can use smaller nozzles to fill the shells with different creams and ganaches.

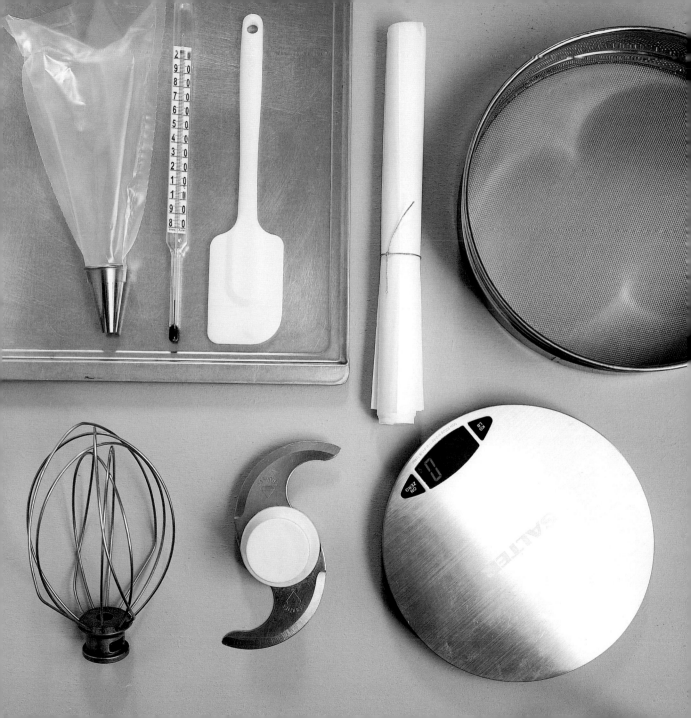

You will need…

Ground almonds

The exact make of ground almonds is not important, just use the first pack you find in the baking aisle of the supermarket. They will work perfectly well.

Sugars

Equal quantities of icing sugar and ground almonds are used to make the 'base' for macaroons.

Caster sugar is used to make the syrup used in the meringue. This type of meringue, made with cooked sugar syrup, is called Italian meringue.

Egg whites

The longer in advance the egg whites are separated, the faster they will become stiff when whisked. Of course, this doesn't mean you should separate them four days before making your macaroons; just prepare them the day before and leave them at room temperature in an airtight container.

Food colouring

Food colourings come in powders, pastes or liquid. I use pastes to colour my mixes before cooking. They are ideal and their intensity is astonishing. You should therefore be careful with your quantities! Using more or less colouring will allow you to vary the colours of your macaroons but watch out. Sometimes one drop too many can change the consistency of your mixture and that could be disastrous! I also use metallic powders after cooking, to obtain subtler and more chic results. Years ago these were very unusual and rarely used products. Now they have become indispensable when making macaroons. They are readily available online.

Other decorations

Sweets, silver balls, sugared almonds, crystallised flowers, flavoured sugars and gold and silver leaf can all add a special touch to your macaroons.

The basics: how to make macaroons in 10 steps

Preparation time: 40 minutes +
1 hour drying time

Cooking time: 13 minutes for mini
macaroons (around 3 cm/1¼
inches in diameter), 15 minutes
for larger macaroons (around
8 cm/3¼ inches in diameter)

Makes around 50 mini macaroons
or 25 larger ones

200 g (7 oz) icing sugar
200 g (7 oz) ground almonds
80 ml (2¾ fl oz) water
200 g (7 oz) caster sugar
2 x 80 g (2¾ oz) egg whites
food colouring of your choice

The base
Mix the icing sugar and ground
almonds together thoroughly
until you have a fine, even
powder. Sieve and set aside.

The syrup
In a saucepan, bring the water
and the caster sugar to the boil.
Use a thermometer to ensure
that the temperature of the
syrup does not exceed 110°C
(230°F). This is very important.

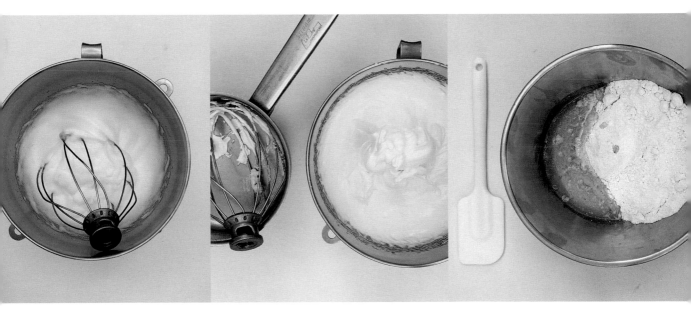

The egg whites

Whisk half the egg whites until they form soft peaks – not too stiff.

The meringue

Decrease the speed of the whisk, then, still whisking, pour the sugar syrup over the egg whites in a thin line. Continue whisking until the mixture has almost cooled, this will take a while and will be easier in a food processor.

The almond paste

Mix the other half of the egg whites (unbeaten) with the sugar and almond base to get a thick paste.

How to make macaroons in 10 steps

Colouring
I add the food colouring to the almond paste to allow me to mix the colour in well without overworking the meringue mix (as this can sometimes have disastrous consequences).

The macaroon mix
Add a little of the meringue to the almond paste with a flexible spatula and stir in with regular motions from the bottom towards the top and from the edges towards the centre of the bowl. Add the rest of the meringue in one go and mix in gently. This is a crucial step: it is the art of making macaroons. The consistency of the macaroon mix should be smooth, even and runny.

Piping
Fill a piping bag with macaroon mix and pipe small even discs of mix on to a tray covered with greaseproof paper. Lightly tap the bottom of the tray on the work surface to remove any small air bubbles. Put the tray aside for 1 hour to allow the shells to dry, then bake in a preheated oven for 15 minutes at 145°C s(fan oven 125°C), Gas Mark 1 ½.

Stop!

Immediately on taking the macaroon shells out of the oven, slide the greaseproof paper on to a lightly dampened work surface. This will stop them over cooking and make them easier to remove from the paper.

Results

The shells should be glossy and smooth with a good colour. If this is not the case, turn to page 54, 'Trouble shooting', to find out what went wrong, or improvise a clever recipe using 'recycled' macaroons!

Fillings... for every taste

Chocolate ganache The chocolate macaroon has always been, and will always be, an essential in patisserie. Since they're good dark and bitter, with milk chocolate or with chocolate chips, a good recipe for chocolate ganache is indispensable.

White chocolate ganache with fruit White chocolate ganache is the ideal base for making fillings with soft, gooey fruit. Its sweetness creates an excellent balance with whole fruits such as blueberries and blackberries, or with coulis made from passion fruit, strawberries, apricots, etc.

Creams In many recipes, I use a light cream (crème mousseline). I find that the light, moussy texture goes perfectly with the crisp macaroon shells. Buttercreams are outdated.

Easy alternatives Lemon curd, caramel and Nutella are all ready-made fillings that you can find in the shops. Marmalade and jams are perfect for filling fruity macaroons

There are no rules about which fillings to use. The examples in this book are just suggestions, so feel free to let your imagination run wild and create your own macaroons – each more impressive than the last.

Finally...

Everybody likes to eat macaroons, but some sort of myth makes us believe that making them is difficult and reserved for a small initiated elite. In this book, we have put all our efforts into proving the opposite... Certainly, a few tools and a few tricks of the trade are necessary, together with a lot of self control and patience (yes I know it's very annoying to see one, two or three batches fail miserably). But you can make as many mistakes with choux pastry or home-made millefeuille as macaroons... so enough said! The most important thing is to enjoy yourself, so let yourself be guided by your imagination. Have fun!

There! No more excuses, now let's get started...

Macaroons from Nancy & Amaretti

Macaroons from Nancy
Preparation time: 15 minutes + 30 minutes drying
Cooking time: 15 minutes
Makes around 45 macaroons

250 g (9 oz) ground almonds
320 g (11¼ oz) icing sugar
3 drops of vanilla extract
4 egg whites, roughly beaten

Mix the ground almonds and the icing sugar together and add the vanilla extract. Add the roughly beaten egg whites and mix to a smooth, dense paste.

Stick a sheet of greaseproof paper to a baking tray with four small dabs of macaroon mix at each corner. Place small, evenly shaped and sized discs at regular intervals across the tray. Tap the bottom of the tray lightly on the work surface and leave to dry slowly at room temperature for half an hour.

Preheat the oven to 180°C (fan oven 160°C), Gas Mark 4. Put the macaroons in the oven and immediately lower the temperature to 150°C (fan oven 130°C), Gas Mark 2. Cook for 15 minutes; the shells should be lightly golden.

Lightly slide the greaseproof paper on to a moist work surface to stop the macaroons cooking any further, then remove the macaroons with a metal spatula.

Tip: The macaroons will keep in an airtight container for 8–10 days.

Amaretti
Preparation time: 15 minutes
Cooking time: 12 minutes
Makes around 35 amaretti

200g (7 oz) ground almonds
150 g (5½ oz) icing sugar, plus a little for decoration
1 egg white
1 teaspoon bitter almond extract
1 dessertspoon amaretto liqueur

Mix together the ground almonds and icing sugar, then add the egg white, almond extract and the amaretto. Mix vigorously to a smooth paste.

Preheat the oven to 180°C (fan oven 160°C), Gas Mark 4.

Make walnut-sized balls of the paste and place them 5 cm (2 inches) apart on a baking tray covered with a sheet of greaseproof paper.

Lightly pinch the top of each ball to make little points and put straight into the oven. Cook for 12 minutes and sprinkle with icing sugar as soon as they come out of the oven.

Vanilla macaroons

Preparation time: 50 minutes
 + 1 hour drying
Cooking time: 13 minutes
Makes around 50 mini macaroons

200 g (7 oz) ground almonds
200 g (7 oz) icing sugar
80 ml (2¾ fl oz) water
200 g (7 oz) caster sugar
2 x 80 g (2¾ oz) egg whites
white food colouring (optional)

Vanilla filling
500 ml (18 fl oz) milk
1 vanilla pod
6 egg yolks
125 g (4½ oz) caster sugar
20 g (¾ oz) plain flour
20 g (¾ oz) cornflour
80 g (2¾ oz) butter, cut into small
 pieces

The day before, prepare the vanilla filling. Warm the milk over a low heat with half the vanilla pod (keep the other half for the macaroons). In a bowl, beat the egg yolks and the sugar together, then add the flour and the cornflour and beat again. Pour the warmed milk into the mixture then put it back over the low heat, stirring constantly for around 3–4 minutes until thick. Take off the heat and mix in the butter until melted. Leave to cool, put in an airtight container and store in the fridge.

Mix then sieve the ground almonds and icing sugar. Set aside.

In a saucepan, bring the water and the caster sugar to the boil. Without mixing, make sure the temperature does not exceed 110°C (230°F).

Whisk half the egg whites to soft peaks, increasing the speed of the whisk once the temperature of the syrup passes 100°C (210°F). Once the syrup reaches 110°C (230°F), take it off the heat and pour in a thin stream on to the whisked egg whites. Beat the meringue mix until it has almost cooled.

Meanwhile, mix the unbeaten egg whites with the almond base to get a thick paste. Add any food colouring.

With a spatula, mix around a third of the meringue with the almond paste to loosen it a little, then add the rest of the meringue and fold in carefully.

Fill a piping bag with the macaroon mix. Stick a sheet of greaseproof paper to a baking tray with four small dabs of macaroon mix at each corner. Make small, evenly shaped and sized discs at regular intervals across the tray. Tap the bottom of the tray lightly on the work surface and leave to dry slowly at room temperature for an hour.

Preheat the oven to 145°C (fan oven 125°C), Gas Mark 1½.

Cook the macaroons for 13 minutes. Immediately on taking them out of the oven, slide the greaseproof paper and shells on to a moistened worktop. This will help the shells detach from the greaseproof paper more easily.

With a piping bag, fill half the shells with the vanilla cream then sandwich together with the remaining shells.

Chocolate macaroons

Preparation time: 40 minutes
+ 1 hour drying
Cooking time: 13 minutes
Makes around 50 mini macaroons

180 g (6¼ oz) ground almonds
200 g (7 oz) icing sugar
30 g (1 oz) cocoa powder
80 ml (2¾ fl oz) water
200 g (7 oz) caster sugar
2 x 80 g (2¾ oz) egg whites
brown food colouring

Chocolate ganache
250 g (9 oz) dark chocolate, broken
into pieces
200 ml (7 oz) single cream
70 g (2½ oz) butter, cut into small
cubes
3 drops of coffee extract

The day before, make the chocolate ganache. Place the chocolate in a mixing bowl. Bring the cream to the boil, pour over the chocolate and mix until the chocolate has melted and mixed with the cream. Add the butter to the mixture with the coffee extract. Stir until the butter has melted. Leave to cool at room temperature then set aside in the fridge.

Mix then sieve the almonds, icing sugar and cocoa powder for the base. Set aside.

In a saucepan, bring the water and the caster sugar to the boil. Without mixing, make sure the temperature does not exceed 110°C (230°F).

Whisk half the egg whites to soft peaks, increasing the speed of the whisk once the temperature of the syrup passes 100°C (210°F). Once the syrup reaches 110°C (230°F), take it off the heat and pour in a thin stream on to the whisked egg whites. Beat the meringue mix until it has almost cooled.

Meanwhile, mix the unbeaten egg whites with the almond base to get a thick paste.

Divide the paste into three and add the brown food colouring, adding more or less to produce three different coloured pastes.

With a spatula, mix around a third of the meringue with the almond pastes to loosen a little, then add the rest of the meringue and fold in carefully.

Fill three piping bags with the macaroon mixtures. Stick a sheet of greaseproof paper to a baking tray with four small dabs of macaroon mix at each corner. Make small, evenly shaped and sized discs at regular intervals across the tray. Tap the bottom of the tray lightly on the work surface and leave to dry slowly at room temperature for an hour.

Preheat the oven to 145°C (fan oven 125°C), Gas Mark 1½.

Cook the macaroons for 13 minutes. Immediately on taking them out of the oven, slide the greaseproof paper and shells on to a moistened worktop. This will help the shells detach from the greaseproof paper more easily.

With a piping bag, fill half the shells with ganache then sandwich together with the remaining shells.

Strawberry and raspberry macaroons

Preparation time: 40 minutes
+ 1 hour drying
Cooking time: 13 minutes
Makes around 50 mini macaroons

For the macaroon mix, see recipe
on pages 8–11
red and pink food colouring
edible silver powder (optional)

Raspberry filling
80 g (2¾ oz) caster sugar
300 g (10½ oz) raspberries
30 g (1 oz) pectin

Strawberry filling
400 g (14 oz) strawberries
juice of half a lemon
150 g (5½ oz) caster sugar
40 g (1½ oz) pectin

Use the basic macaroon recipe (pages 8–11) for the almond paste, then divide it into two portions. Lightly colour one half with the red colouring and colour the other half more strongly with pink colouring. Follow the basic recipe to make the meringue mixture.

Divide the meringue between the two bowls of almond paste and mix carefully.

Fill two piping bags with the different coloured mixtures. Cover a baking tray with greaseproof paper and stick down with a disc of macaroon mix in each corner. Make small discs regularly and well-spaced across the tray. Lightly tap the bottom of the tray against the work surface and leave to dry at room temperature for one hour.

Preheat the oven to 145°C (fan oven 125°C), Gas Mark 1½.

Cook the macaroon shells for 13 minutes. Immediately on taking them out of the oven, slide the greaseproof paper and shells on to a moistened worktop. This will help the shells detach from the greaseproof paper more easily.

For the raspberry filling, dissolve the sugar with a little water over a low heat. Add the raspberries and leave to cook for just 2–3 minutes. Add the pectin, mix well and put in the fridge.

For the strawberry filling, wash the strawberries then remove the stalks. Cut half of the fruit into small pieces and set aside. Mix the other half with the lemon juice, sugar and 2 dessertspoons of water. Add the pectin. Heat gently until the pectin is dissolved then pour the mixture on to the chopped strawberries. Mix well and put in the fridge.

At the last moment, just before serving, assemble the macaroons. Using your fingertips, dust some of the shells with the silver powder, if you wish. With the aid of a teaspoon, fill the darker pink shells with the raspberry mix and the paler ones with the strawberry filling.

Tip: You can use strawberry and raspberry jams instead of the home-made fillings if you want to save time. Just add a few small pieces of fresh strawberry or raspberry.

Pistachio macaroons

Preparation time: 50 minutes
 + 1 hour drying
Cooking time: 13 minutes
Makes around 50 mini macaroons

200 g (7 oz) ground almonds
200 g (7 oz) icing sugar
80 ml (2¾ fl oz) water
200 g (7 oz) caster sugar
2 x 80 g (2¾ oz) egg whites
green and yellow food colouring

Pistachio cream
120 g (4¼ oz) unsalted pistachios,
 very finely chopped (+ 2 drops of
 green food colouring if necessary)
1 dessertspoon barley malt syrup
220 g (7¾ oz) butter, softened
125 g (4½ oz) icing sugar
70 g (2½ oz) ground almonds

Mix then sieve the ground almonds and icing sugar. Set aside.

In a saucepan, bring the water and the caster sugar to the boil. Without mixing, make sure the temperature does not exceed 110°C (230°F).

Whisk half the egg whites to soft peaks, increasing the speed of the whisk once the temperature of the syrup passes 100°C (210°F). Once the syrup reaches 110°C (230°F), take it off the heat and pour in a thin stream on to the whisked egg whites. Beat the meringue mix until it has almost cooled.

Meanwhile, mix the unbeaten egg whites with the almond base to get a thick paste. Add some green food colouring and a little yellow until pistachio-coloured.

With a spatula, mix around a third of the meringue with the almond paste to loosen it a little, then add the rest of the meringue and fold in carefully.

Fill a piping bag with the macaroon mix. Stick a sheet of greaseproof paper to a baking tray with four small dabs of macaroon mix at each corner. Make small, evenly shaped and sized discs at regular intervals across the tray. Tap the bottom of the tray lightly on the work surface and leave to dry slowly at room temperature for an hour.

Preheat the oven to 145°C (fan oven 125°C), Gas Mark 1½.

Cook the macaroons for 13 minutes. Immediately on taking them out of the oven, slide the greaseproof paper and shells on to a moistened worktop. This will help the shells detach from the greaseproof paper more easily.

Make the pistachio cream. Mix the pistachios with the barley syrup to get a smooth pistachio paste (add some green food colouring if necessary). Beat the butter vigorously with a mixer or electric whisk until it has the consistency of very smooth ointment. Add the icing sugar and beat again. Mix in the ground almonds and the pistachio paste and beat for several minutes to make the cream airy and light.

With a piping bag, fill half the shells with pistachio cream then sandwich together with the remaining shells.

Salted caramel macaroons

Preparation time: 50 minutes
  + 1 hour drying
Cooking time: 13 minutes
Makes around 50 mini macaroons

200 g (7 oz) ground almonds
200 g (7 oz) icing sugar
80 ml (2¾ fl oz) water
200 g (7 oz) caster sugar
2 x 80 g (2¾ oz) egg whites
caramel food colouring or coffee
  extract mixed with 2 drops of
  yellow food colouring

Salted caramel
250 g (9 oz) icing sugar
80 ml (2¾ fl oz) water
120 g (4¼ oz) full fat crème fraîche
200 g (7 oz) salted butter, cut into
  small cubes

The day before, prepare the caramel. Over a low heat, dissolve the sugar in the water. Without mixing them too much, watch the sugar until it turns a light brown colour. Add the crème fraîche, little by little, mixing with a spatula to stop the caramel cooking (watch out for splashes). Once the crème fraîche is well mixed in, use a thermometer to monitor the temperature. As soon as the caramel reaches 108°C (226°F), remove it from the heat and add the butter. Mix or whisk until the caramel is smooth. Put in a bowl and leave in the fridge.

Mix then sieve together the ground almonds and icing sugar. Set aside.

In a saucepan, bring the water and the caster sugar to the boil. Without mixing, make sure the temperature does not exceed 110°C (230°F).

Whisk half the egg whites to soft peaks, increasing the speed of the whisk once the temperature of the syrup passes 100°C (210°F). Once the syrup reaches 110°C (230°F), take it off the heat and pour in a thin stream on to the whisked egg whites. Beat the meringue mix until it has almost cooled.

Meanwhile, mix the unbeaten egg whites with the almond base to get a thick paste. Add the coffee extract and/or the colouring to get a pale caramel colour.

With a spatula, mix around a third of the meringue with the almond paste to loosen it a little, then add the rest of the meringue and fold in carefully.

Fill a piping bag with the macaroon mix. Stick a sheet of greaseproof paper to a baking tray with four small dabs of macaroon mix at each corner. Make small, evenly shaped and sized balls at regular intervals across the tray. Tap the bottom of the tray lightly on the work surface and leave to dry at room temperature for an hour.

Preheat the oven to 145°C (fan oven 125°C), Gas Mark 1½.

Cook the macaroons for 13 minutes. Immediately on taking them out of the oven, slide the greaseproof paper and shells on to a moistened worktop. This will help the shells detach from the greaseproof paper more easily.

With a piping bag, fill half the shells with caramel then sandwich together with the remaining shells.

Coffee macaroons

Preparation time: 50 minutes
+ 1 hour drying
Cooking time: 13 minutes
Makes around 50 mini macaroons

180 g (6¼ oz) ground almonds
200 g (7 oz) icing sugar
80 ml (2¾ fl oz) water
200 g (7 oz) caster sugar
2 x 80 g (2¾ oz) egg whites
a few drops of coffee extract

Coffee cream
250 g (9 oz) butter, softened
140 g (5 oz) icing sugar
160 g (5½ oz) ground almonds
a little coffee extract or around 20 g
(¾ oz) instant coffee

Mix then sieve together the ground almonds and icing sugar. Set aside.

In a saucepan, bring the water and the caster sugar to the boil. Without mixing, make sure the temperature does not exceed 110°C (230°F).

Whisk half the egg whites to soft peaks, increasing the speed of the whisk once the temperature of the syrup passes 100°C (210°F). Once the syrup reaches 110°C (230°F), take it off the heat and pour in a thin stream on to the whisked egg whites. Beat the meringue mix until it has almost cooled.

Meanwhile, mix the unbeaten egg whites with the almond base to get a thick paste. Add the coffee extract.

With a spatula, mix around a third of the meringue with the almond paste to loosen it a little, then add the rest of the meringue and fold in carefully.

Fill a piping bag with the macaroon mix. Stick a sheet of greaseproof paper to a baking tray with four small dabs of macaroon mix at each corner. Make small, evenly shaped and sized balls at regular intervals across the tray. Tap the bottom of

the tray lightly on the work surface and leave to dry slowly at room temperature for an hour.

Preheat the oven to 145°C (fan oven 125°C), Gas Mark 1½.

Cook the macaroons for 13 minutes. Immediately on taking them out of the oven, slide the greaseproof paper and shells on to a moistened worktop. This will help the shells detach from the greaseproof paper more easily.

Make the coffee cream. Beat the soft butter vigorously with a mixer or electric whisk until it has the consistency of very smooth ointment. Add the icing sugar and beat again. Mix in the ground almonds and the coffee extract and beat for several minutes to make the cream airy and light. Test and adjust the amount of coffee according to taste.

With a piping bag, fill half the shells with the coffee cream then sandwich together with the remaining shells.

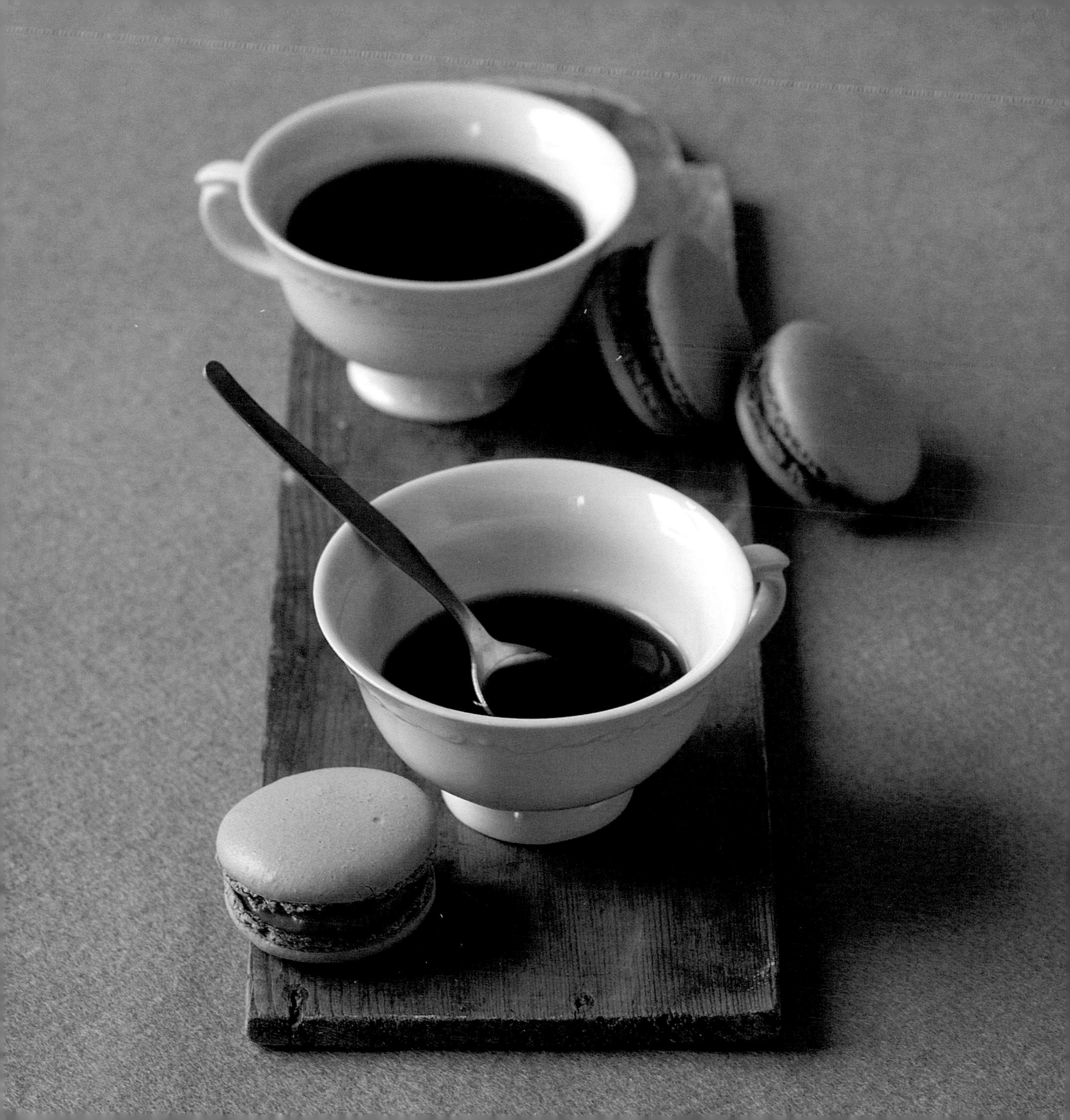

Double chocolate macaroons

Preparation time: 50 minutes
+ 1 hour drying
Cooking time: 13 minutes
Makes around 50 mini macaroons

180 g (6¼ oz) ground almonds
200 g (7 oz) icing sugar
30 g (1 oz) cocoa powder
80 ml (2¾ fl oz) water
200 g (7 oz) caster sugar
2 x 80 g (2¾ oz) egg whites

Chocolate ganache
220 g (7¾ oz) dark chocolate (70%
minimum cocoa solids), broken
into pieces
200 ml (7 fl oz) single cream
20 g (¾ oz) icing sugar
50 g (1¾ oz) butter, cubed

Decoration
iridescent edible bronze powder
(optional)
125 g (4½ oz) dark chocolate
1 teaspoon of neutral oil such as
groundnut or sunflower

The day before make the chocolate ganache. Place the chocolate in a mixing bowl. Bring the cream and the sugar to the boil, pour over the chocolate and mix until the chocolate has melted and blended with the cream. Add the butter to the mixture and stir until melted. Leave to cool at room temperature then set aside in the fridge.

Follow the basic macaroon recipe (pages 8–11), adding the cocoa powder to the base.

Fill a piping bag with the macaroon mix. Stick a sheet of greaseproof paper to a baking tray with four small dabs of macaroon mix at each corner. Make small, evenly shaped and sized balls at regular intervals across the tray. Tap the bottom of the tray lightly on the work surface and leave to dry slowly at room temperature for an hour.

Preheat the oven to 145°C (fan oven 125°C), Gas Mark 1½.

Cook the macaroons for 13 minutes. Immediately on taking them out of the oven, slide the greaseproof paper and shells on to a moistened worktop. This will help the shells detach from the greaseproof paper more easily.

Using your fingertips, dust some of the shells with the iridescent powder, if using. With a piping bag, fill half the shells with the chocolate ganache, then sandwich together with the remaining shells. Space them out on a baking tray that has been covered with greaseproof paper.

Melt the dark chocolate with the oil in a bowl placed over a saucepan of boiling water, or melt very carefully in the microwave.

Cut a piece of greaseproof paper into a right-angled 20 x 30 cm (8 x 12 inch) triangle. Take the right angle between thumb and index finger, roll the paper around the two fingers to make a tight cone, then fold the other two corners inside the cone. Fill halfway with the melted chocolate then cut the tip off. Squeeze thin stripes of chocolate back and forth across the macaroons. Put in the fridge for a few minutes to set the chocolate.

Lime macaroons

Preparation time: 40 minutes
+ 1 hour drying
Cooking time: 13 minutes
Makes around 50 mini macaroons

200 g (7 oz) ground almonds
200 g (7 oz) icing sugar
80 ml (2¾ fl oz) water
200 g (7 oz) caster sugar
2 x 80 g (2¾ oz) egg whites
green and yellow food colouring

Lime cream
200 ml (7 fl oz) lime juice
3 whole eggs
6 egg yolks
75 g (2¾ oz) caster sugar
110 g (3¾ oz) butter
125 g (4½ oz) white chocolate,
broken into pieces

The day before, make the lime cream. Heat the lime juice over a low heat. In a bowl, beat the 3 eggs and the egg yolks with the sugar. Add the hot lime juice then return the mixture to the heat, stirring constantly until it thickens. Mix in the butter and the white chocolate. Leave to cool then set aside in the fridge.

Mix then sieve together the ground almonds and icing sugar. Set aside.

In a saucepan, bring the water and the caster sugar to the boil. Without mixing, make sure the temperature does not exceed 110°C (230°F).

Whisk half the egg whites to soft peaks, increasing the speed of the whisk once the temperature of the syrup passes 100°C (210°F). Once the syrup reaches 110°C (230°F), take it off the heat and pour in a thin stream on to the whisked egg whites. Beat the meringue mix until it has almost cooled.

Meanwhile, mix the unbeaten egg whites with the almond base to get a thick paste. Add some green food colouring and a little yellow until lime green in colour.

With a spatula, mix around a third of the meringue with the almond paste to loosen it a little then add the rest of the meringue and fold in carefully.

Fill a piping bag with the macaroon mix. Stick a sheet of greaseproof paper to a baking tray with four small dabs of macaroon mix at each corner. Make small, evenly shaped and sized balls at regular intervals across the tray. Tap the bottom of the tray lightly on the work surface and leave to dry slowly at room temperature for an hour.

Preheat the oven to 145°C (fan oven 125°C), Gas Mark 1½.

Cook the macaroons for 13 minutes. Immediately on taking them out of the oven, slide the greaseproof paper and shells on to a moistened worktop. This will help the shells detach from the greaseproof paper more easily.

With a piping bag, fill half the shells with the lime cream then sandwich together with the remaining shells.

Tip: To save time, use ready-made lemon curd instead of the lime cream.

Honey macaroons

Preparation time: 40 minutes
+ 1 hour drying
Cooking time: 13 minutes
Makes around 50 mini macaroons

200 g (7 oz) ground almonds
200 g (7 oz) icing sugar
80 ml (2¾ fl oz) water
140 g (5 oz) caster sugar
60 g (2 oz) honey
2 x 80 g (2¾ oz) egg whites
caramel food colouring
iridescent edible bronze or copper
powder

Honey cream
2 egg yolks
60 g (2 oz) honey
250 g (9 oz) mascarpone
50 g (1¾ oz) pollen de fleurs
(optional)

Mix then sieve together the ground almonds and icing sugar. Set aside.

In a saucepan, bring the water, caster sugar and honey to the boil. Without mixing, make sure the temperature does not exceed 110°C (230°F).

Whisk half the egg whites to soft peaks, increasing the speed of the whisk once the temperature of the syrup passes 100°C (210°F). Once the syrup reaches 110°C (230°F), take it off the heat and pour in a thin stream on to the whisked egg whites. Beat the meringue mix until it has almost cooled.

Meanwhile, mix the unbeaten egg whites with the almond base to get a thick paste. Add a little caramel food colouring.

With a spatula, mix around a third of the meringue with the almond paste to loosen it a little then add the rest of the meringue and fold in carefully.

Fill a piping bag with the macaroon mix. Stick a sheet of greaseproof paper to a baking tray with four small dabs of macaroon mix at each corner. Make small, evenly shaped and sized discs at regular intervals across the tray. Tap the bottom of the tray lightly on the work surface and leave to dry slowly at room temperature for an hour.

Preheat the oven to 145°C (fan oven 125°C), Gas Mark 1½.

Cook the macaroons for 13 minutes. Immediately on taking them out of the oven, slide the greaseproof paper and shells on to a moistened worktop. This will help the shells detach from the greaseproof paper more easily. Using your fingertips, dust the shells with the iridescent powder.

Make the cream. In a bowl, lightly whisk the egg yolks and the honey then add the mascarpone and beat again. Gently mix in the pollen de fleurs, if using.

With a piping bag, fill half the shells with the honey cream then sandwich together with the remaining shells.

Blackcurrant and white chocolate macaroons

Preparation time: 40 minutes
+ 1 hour resting
Cooking time: 13 minutes
Makes around 50 mini macaroons

200 g (7 oz) ground almonds
200 g (7 oz) icing sugar
80 ml (2¾ fl oz) water
200 g (7 oz) caster sugar
2 x 80 g (2¾ oz) egg whites
pink and purple food colouring

Chocolate and blackcurrant ganache

350 g (12 oz) white chocolate, broken into pieces
200 ml (7 fl oz) single cream
50 g (1¾ oz) butter, cut into small cubes
125 g (4½ oz) fresh or frozen blackcurrants

The day before, make the white chocolate and blackcurrant ganache. Place the chocolate in a bowl. Bring the cream to the boil, pour over the chocolate and mix until it is completely melted. Stir the butter into the mix until melted. Leave to cool at room temperature. Stir the fruit into the ganache. Keep in the fridge.

Mix then sieve the ground almonds and icing sugar. Set aside.

In a saucepan, bring the water and the caster sugar to the boil. Without mixing, make sure the temperature does not exceed 110°C (230°F).

Whisk half the egg whites to soft peaks, increasing the speed of the whisk once the temperature of the syrup passes 100°C (210°F). Once the syrup reaches 110°C (230°F), take it off the heat and pour in a thin stream on to the whisked egg whites. Beat the meringue mix until it has almost cooled.

Meanwhile, mix the unbeaten egg whites with the almond base to get a thick paste. Add some purple food colouring lightened with a little of the pink colouring.

With a spatula, mix around a third of the meringue with the almond paste to loosen it a little then add the rest of the meringue and fold in carefully.

Fill a piping bag with the macaroon mix. Stick a sheet of greaseproof paper to a baking tray with four small dabs of macaroon mix at each corner. Make small, evenly shaped and sized balls at regular intervals across the tray. Tap the bottom of the tray lightly on the work surface and leave to dry slowly at room temperature for an hour.

Preheat the oven to 145°C (fan oven 125°C), Gas Mark 1½.

Cook the macaroons for 13 minutes. Immediately on taking them out of the oven, slide the greaseproof paper and shells on to a moistened worktop. This will help the shells detach from the greaseproof paper more easily.

With a piping bag, fill half the shells with the cold ganache then sandwich together with the remaining shells.

Apple and cinnamon/Pear and ginger/ Coconut and passion fruit macaroons

Preparation time: 40 minutes
  + 1 hour drying
Cooking time: 13 minutes
Makes around 15 mini macaroons
  of each flavour

For the macaroon mix, see recipe
  on pages 8–11

**Coconut and passion fruit
  macaroons**
white food colouring
100 g (3½ oz) grated coconut
1 pineapple
2 passion fruit
75 g (2¾ oz) caster sugar
15 g (½ oz) pectin

Pear and ginger macaroons
white food colouring
orange powder
3 pears
20 g (¾ oz) fresh ginger
75 g (2¾ oz) caster sugar
15 g (½ oz) pectin

Apple and cinnamon macaroons
jade green and lemon yellow food
  colouring
3 apples
75 g (2¾ oz) caster sugar
½ teaspoon cinnamon
15 g (½ oz) pectin

Follow the basic macaroon recipe from pages 8–11. Divide the mix into three. Colour each third according to the macaroon flavours. Leave to dry for an hour.

For the Coconut and passion fruit macaroons, sprinkle with grated coconut just before cooking.

Cook at 145°C (fan oven 125°C), Gas Mark 1½ for 13 minutes.

For the Pear and ginger macaroons, delicately dust the shells with orange powder after cooking.

Peel the fruit and the ginger and cut them into small pieces. Scoop out the passion fruit seeds.

For each recipe, cook the fruit in the sugar with any spices and leave to stew gently.

Add the pectin, mix well and keep in the fridge.

Assemble the macaroons by filling them with the respective fruit just before serving.

Sesame and tahini macaroons

Preparation time: 40 minutes
  + 1 hour drying
Cooking time: 13 minutes
Makes around 50 mini macaroons

200 g (7 oz) ground almonds
200 g (7 oz) icing sugar
80 ml (2¾ fl oz) water
200 g (7 oz) caster sugar
2 x 80 g (2¾ oz) egg whites
1 dessertspoon white food
  colouring
iridescent edible white powder

Tahini filling
1 medium-sized jar tahini
2 dessertspoons plain fromage frais
sesame seeds, toasted

Mix then sieve the ground almonds and icing sugar. Set aside.

In a saucepan, bring the water and the caster sugar to the boil. Without mixing, make sure the temperature does not exceed 110°C (230°F).

Whisk half the egg whites to soft peaks, increasing the speed of the whisk once the temperature of the syrup passes 100°C (210°F). Once the syrup reaches 110°C (230°F), take it off the heat and pour in a thin stream on to the whisked egg whites. Beat the meringue mix until it has almost cooled.

Meanwhile, mix the unbeaten egg whites with the almond base to get a thick paste. Add a little of the white food colouring.

With a spatula, mix around a third of the meringue with the almond paste to loosen it a little then add the rest of the meringue and fold in carefully.

Fill a piping bag with the macaroon mix. Stick a sheet of greaseproof paper to a baking tray with four small dabs of macaroon mix at each corner. Make small, evenly shaped and sized discs at regular intervals across the tray. Tap the bottom of the tray lightly on the work surface and leave to dry slowly at room temperature for an hour.

Preheat the oven to 145°C (fan oven 125°C), Gas Mark 1½.

Cook the macaroons for 13 minutes. Immediately on taking them out of the oven, slide the greaseproof paper and shells on to a moistened worktop. This will help the shells detach from the greaseproof paper more easily.

Lightly beat the tahini with the fromage frais to loosen it and make it runnier.

Using your fingertips, dust a third of the shells with the iridescent powder. Fill half the shells with the tahini cream, then sandwich together with the other half. Roll the edges of the macaroons in the sesame seeds.

Liquorice and violet macaroons

Preparation time: 40 minutes
  + 1 hour drying
Cooking time: 13 minutes
Makes around 50 mini macaroons

For the macaroon mix, see recipe
  on pages 8–11
purple food colouring

Liquorice violet cream
2 egg yolks
30 g (1 oz) caster sugar
250 g (9 oz) mascarpone
a few drops of violet flavouring
50 g (1¾ oz) crystallised violets
30 g (1 oz) liquorice

Follow the basic macaroon recipe on pages 8–11, dividing the almond base between three bowls and adding varying amounts of food colouring to get three different shades of purple. Divide the meringue between the three bowls and mix carefully. Fill a piping bag with each mixture.

Stick a sheet of greaseproof paper to a baking tray with four small dabs of macaroon mix at each corner. Using each piping bag in turn, make small, evenly shaped and sized discs at regular intervals across the tray. Tap the bottom of the tray lightly on the work surface and leave to dry slowly at room temperature for an hour.

Preheat the oven to 145°C (fan oven 125°C), Gas Mark 1½.

Cook the macaroons for 13 minutes. Immediately on taking them out of the oven, slide the greaseproof paper and shells on to a moistened worktop. This will help the shells detach from the greaseproof paper more easily.

Make the liquorice violet cream. In a bowl, lightly beat the egg yolks and the sugar together, then add the mascarpone and the violet flavouring and beat again. Add some small pieces of violet and liquorice.

With a piping bag, fill half the shells with the chilled cream then sandwich together with the remaining shells.

Raspberry and aniseed macaroons

Preparation time: 40 minutes
+ 1 hour drying
Cooking time: 13 minutes
Makes around 50 mini macaroons

For the macaroon mix, see recipe
on pages 8–11
green food colouring
raspberry pink food colouring
1 teaspoon aniseed

Aniseed cream
250 ml (9 fl oz) milk
2 teaspoons aniseed
3 egg yolks
60 g (2 oz) caster sugar
15 g (½ oz) plain flour
40 g (1½ oz) butter
a dash of pastis

Raspberry jam
80 g (2¾ oz) caster sugar
50 ml (1¾ fl oz) water
300 g (10½ oz) raspberries
25 g (1 oz) pectin

Follow the basic macaroon recipe on pages 8–11, dividing the almond base between two bowls and colouring half with a very little green food colouring and the other half more generously with pink. Fill a piping bag with each.

Stick a sheet of greaseproof paper to a baking tray by dabbing macaroon mix into the four corners of the tray. Using each piping bag in turn, make small, evenly shaped and sized discs at regular intervals across the tray. Tap the bottom of the tray lightly on the work surface and leave to dry slowly at room temperature for an hour.

Preheat the oven to 145°C (fan oven 125°C), Gas Mark 1½. Sprinkle the green shells with the aniseed and cook the macaroons for 13 minutes.

For the aniseed cream, warm the milk over a low heat with the 2 teaspoons of aniseed. In a bowl, beat the eggs and the sugar, then add the flour and beat again. Pour the aniseed milk through a very fine sieve into the mixture and re-heat over a low heat, stirring constantly for around 2 minutes. Add the butter. Add the pastis, according to taste, and put in the fridge in an airtight container.

For the jam, dissolve the sugar in the water over a low heat then add the raspberries and leave to cook for 2–3 minutes. Add the pectin, mix well and keep in the fridge.

To make the macaroons, fill half the aniseed shells with the raspberry jam and half the raspberry shells with the aniseed cream then sandwich together with the remaining shells.

Lemon and bergamot macaroons

Preparation time: 40 minutes
  + 1 hour drying
Cooking time: 13 minutes
Makes around 50 mini macaroons

200 g (7 oz) ground almonds
200 g (7 oz) icing sugar
80 ml (2¾ fl oz) water
200 g (7 oz) caster sugar
2 x 80 g (2¾ oz) egg whites
dark green food colouring

Lemon bergamot cream
150 ml (5¼ fl oz) lemon juice
3 whole eggs
6 egg yolks
75 g (2¾ oz) caster sugar
100 g (3½ oz) butter
125 g (4½ oz) white chocolate,
  broken into pieces
a few drops of bergamot essence

The day before, make the lemon bergamot cream. Warm the lemon juice over a low heat. In a bowl, beat the 3 eggs with the egg yolks and the sugar. Pour the heated lemon juice over the mixture and return to a low heat, stirring constantly for 3–4 minutes until thick. Mix in the butter and the white chocolate. Add three drops of bergamot essence. Keep in an airtight container in the fridge.

Mix then sieve the ground almonds and icing sugar. Set aside.

In a saucepan, bring the water and the caster sugar to the boil. Without mixing, make sure the temperature does not exceed 110°C (230°F).

Whisk half the egg whites to soft peaks, increasing the speed of the whisk once the temperature of the syrup passes 100°C (210°F). Once the syrup reaches 110°C (230°F), take it off the heat and pour in a thin stream on to the whisked egg whites. Beat the meringue mix until it has almost cooled.

Meanwhile, mix the unbeaten egg whites with the almond base to get a thick paste. Add some of the green food colouring.

With a spatula, mix around a third of the meringue with the almond paste to loosen it a little then add the rest of the meringue and fold in carefully.

Fill a piping bag with the macaroon mix. Stick a sheet of greaseproof paper to a baking tray with four small dabs of macaroon mix at each corner. Make small, evenly shaped and sized discs at regular intervals across the tray. Tap the bottom of the tray lightly on the work surface and leave to dry slowly at room temperature for an hour.

Preheat the oven to 145°C (fan oven 125°C), Gas Mark 1½.

Cook the macaroons for 13 minutes. Immediately on taking them out of the oven, slide the greaseproof paper and shells on to a moistened worktop. This will help the shells detach from the greaseproof paper more easily. Sandwich the macaroons together, filling them with the lemon bergamot cream using a piping bag.

Pineapple and saffron macaroons

Preparation time: 40 minutes
  + 1 hour drying
Cooking time: 15 minutes
Makes around 50 mini macaroons

You will need a toothbrush

For the macaroon mix, see recipe
  on pages 8–11
yellow food colouring
powdered saffron
red liquid food colouring

Pineapple filling
2 pineapples
300 g (10½ oz) caster sugar
100 ml (3½ fl oz) water
powdered saffron
30 g (1¼ oz) pectin

Follow the basic macaroon recipe on pages 8–11, colouring the mixture with yellow food colouring and flavouring with a little powdered saffron. Leave to dry at room temperature for an hour then spray the macaroons with red food colouring by dipping a toothbrush in the colouring and flicking the bristles with your thumb. Cook for 15 minutes.

Peel the pineapples and chop into small pieces.

Dissolve the sugar in the water over a low heat, then add the pineapple pieces and a little saffron and leave to cook for 7–8 minutes. Add the pectin, mix well and put in the fridge.

Just before serving, fill half the shells with the pineapple filling using a small spoon, then sandwich with the remaining shells.

Blueberry macaroons (macaroons from Camille)

Preparation time: 40 minutes
  + 1 hour drying
Cooking time: 15 minutes
Makes around 20 large macaroons

200 g (7 oz) ground almonds
200 g (7 oz) icing sugar
80 ml (2¾ fl oz) water
200 g (7 oz) caster sugar
2 x 80 g (2¾ oz) egg whites
purple food colouring

Filling and decoration
good quality blueberry jam
125 g (4½ oz) fresh blueberries
100 g (3½ oz) silver covered
  chocolate dragées

Mix then sieve the ground almonds and icing sugar. Set aside.

In a saucepan, bring the water and the caster sugar to the boil. Without mixing, make sure the temperature does not exceed 110°C (230°F).

Whisk half the egg whites to soft peaks, increasing the speed of the whisk once the temperature of the syrup passes 100°C (210°F). Once the syrup reaches 110°C (230°F), take it off the heat and pour in a thin stream on to the whisked egg whites. Beat the meringue mix until it has almost cooled.

Meanwhile, mix the unbeaten egg whites with the almond base to get a thick paste. Add some of the purple food colouring.

With a spatula, mix around a third of the meringue with the almond paste to loosen it a little then add the rest of the meringue and fold in carefully.

Fill a piping bag with the macaroon mix. Stick a sheet of greaseproof paper to a baking tray with four small dabs of macaroon mix at each corner. Make small, evenly shaped and sized discs at regular intervals across the tray. Tap the bottom of the tray lightly on the work surface and leave to dry slowly at room temperature for an hour.

Preheat the oven to 145°C (fan oven 125°C), Gas Mark 1½.

Cook the macaroons for 15 minutes. Immediately on taking them out of the oven, slide the greaseproof paper and shells on to a moistened worktop. This will help the shells detach from the greaseproof paper more easily. With a spoon, fill half the shells with the blueberry jam then alternate the blueberries and silver dragées around the edges before sandwiching with the remaining macaroon shells.

Rose macaroons with sherbet

Preparation time: 40 minutes
+ 1 hour drying
Cooking time: 15 minutes
Makes around 50 mini macaroons

200 g (7 oz) ground almonds
200 g (7 oz) icing sugar
80 ml (2¾ fl oz) water
200 g (7 oz) caster sugar
2 x 80 g (2¾ oz) egg whites
pink food colouring
a few drops of rose water

Filling and decoration
iridescent edible pink powder
2 egg whites, beaten
some sherbet
rose jam

Mix then sieve the ground almonds and icing sugar. Set aside.

In a saucepan, bring the water and the caster sugar to the boil. Without mixing, make sure the temperature does not exceed 110°C (230°F).

Whisk half the egg whites to soft peaks, increasing the speed of the whisk once the temperature of the syrup passes 100°C (210°F). Once the syrup reaches 110°C (230°F), take it off the heat and pour in a thin stream on to the whisked egg whites. Beat the meringue mix until it has almost cooled.

Meanwhile, mix the unbeaten egg whites with the almond base to get a thick paste. Add some pink food colouring and the rose water.

With a spatula, mix around a third of the meringue with the almond paste to loosen it a little then add the rest of the meringue and fold in carefully.

Fill a piping bag with the macaroon mix. Stick a sheet of greaseproof paper to a baking tray with four small dabs of macaroon mix at each corner. Make small, evenly shaped and sized discs at regular intervals across the tray. Tap the bottom of the tray lightly on the work surface and leave to dry slowly at room temperature for an hour.

Preheat the oven to 145°C (fan oven 125°C), Gas Mark 1½.

Cook the macaroons for 15 minutes. Immediately on taking them out of the oven, slide the greaseproof paper and shells on to a moistened worktop. This will help the shells detach from the greaseproof paper more easily.

Dust a third of the shells with the iridescent pink powder and brush a third with the egg white then sprinkle with sherbet. Fill half the macaroons with rose jam then sandwich together with the remaining shells.

Trouble shooting

This page should help remove the perceived mystery of making macaroons as it will show you that almost all mistakes are down to one of the following reasons…

Beware of pale-coloured macaroons!
Light-coloured macaroons – pink, white, etc. – often brown when cooking. In order to avoid this problem, lower the cooking temperature slightly and leave them in for a few extra minutes.

The shells are flat and have lost their pretty colour
The macaroon mix was over mixed (see page 10), so the beaten egg whites fell and became too liquid.

The shells aren't smooth
The almond and sugar base wasn't well mixed or sieved thoroughly enough.

The shells aren't round
They weren't piped confidently enough. You must be very precise; the piping bag should be held perpendicular to the baking tray and you should move it away with a quick, sharp movement.

The shells are cracked
There are three possible explanations:
1. The oven temperature was too high
2. The paste wasn't mixed well enough (see page 10)
3. The shells were cooked too early so did not have enough time to dry

Solutions...
Try again until you achieve perfect results.

Be inspired by the following pages to make a trifle with macaroon crumbs (page 64), messed up macaroon lollipops (page 56) or a magnificent charlotte of misshapen macaroons (page 66)!

If fewer than half your macaroons were ruined, use the best for the top and save the cracked ones or the least round for the bottom. They'll be too delicious for people to notice anyway.

Macaroon sweets

Preparation time: around
  20 minutes
Refrigeration time: 15 minutes

macaroon shells
chocolate ganache
lollipop sticks
white chocolate
dark chocolate
sugar
glucose
food colouring
chocolate sprinkles
coloured sugar
crystallised flowers

Lay half the shells on a baking tray.

Using a piping bag, fill them with a small blob of chocolate ganache (see the recipe for Chocolate macaroons, page 20), then stick the lollipop sticks lightly in the ganache. Cover with the remaining shells and press lightly to fix the lollipops together.

Melt the white and dark chocolate over simmering water in two separate bowls.

Meanwhile, dissolve the sugar and glucose in water, adding food colouring if you wish (for the method, see the recipe for Saint Honoré, page 68).

Dip a third of the lollipops in the sugar syrup and the rest in the melted chocolates.

Lay the lollipops on greaseproof paper and sprinkle with chocolate sprinkles, coloured sugars or pieces of crystallised flowers.

Put the lollipops in the fridge for around 15 minutes to harden the chocolate.

Chocolate 'terrine'

Preparation time: 50 minutes
+ 30 minutes drying
Cooking time: 15 minutes
Chilling time: 1 hour 30 minutes
Serves 6 or 8 people

For the macaroon mix, see recipe
on pages 8–11
cocoa powder

White chocolate mousse
1 sheet of gelatine
125 ml (4 fl oz) single cream
150 g (5¼ oz) white chocolate,
broken into pieces
125 ml (4 fl oz) whipping cream,
whipped

Dark chocolate icing
300 ml (10 fl oz) water
450 g (1 lb) caster sugar
170 g (6 oz) cocoa powder
10 sheets of gelatine
250 ml (9 fl oz) single cream

Chocolate caramel mousse
50 g (1¾ oz) caster sugar
100 ml (3½ fl oz) single cream
120 g (4¼ oz) dark chocolate,
broken into pieces
3 egg yolks
250 ml (9 fl oz) whipping cream,
whipped

Follow the basic macaroon recipe on pages 8–11. Pipe 12 strips of macaroon mix (the length of your terrine dish) on to the greaseproof paper. Leave to dry at room temperature for 30 minutes.

Preheat the oven to 145°C (fan oven 125°C), Gas Mark 1½.

Cook for 15 minutes. Immediately on taking them out of the oven, slide the greaseproof paper and macaroon strips on to a moistened worktop. Slide the strips of macaroon off the paper, taking care not to break them. Set aside.

For the white chocolate mousse, soften the gelatine sheet in cold water, bring the single cream to the boil, then add the gelatine and pour over the white chocolate. Mix. Mix the whipped cream carefully with the cooled white chocolate cream.

Cover the bottom of your terrine dish with a layer of macaroon strips, then pour over the white chocolate mousse until the dish is filled a third of the way up. Put in the fridge and keep the remaining mousse at room temperature.

For the icing, heat the water and sugar, then add the cocoa powder. Dissolve over a low heat. Soften the gelatine in cold water. In another pan, bring the cream to the boil, add the gelatine, mix, then pour over the cocoa syrup. Leave to cool.

For the chocolate caramel mousse, put the caster sugar in a small saucepan over a low heat until it caramelises. Add the cream and return to the heat to mix it all together. Place the chocolate in a bowl and pour the caramel cream over. Mix well to melt, then add the egg yolks. Add the whipped cream and mix delicately into the chocolate caramel.

Make sure the white chocolate mousse has set well and add another layer of macaroons. Cover with a thin layer of chocolate icing that is warm but not too hot.

Pour on the chocolate caramel mousse and then the rest of the white chocolate mousse. Put in the fridge to chill.

Before serving, finish the terrine with the remaining macaroons and a dusting of cocoa powder.

Paris-Brest

Preparation time: 20 minutes
+ 30 minutes drying
Cooking time: 15 minutes
Serves 4

For the macaroon mix, see recipe
on pages 8–11
brown food colouring
40 g (1½ oz) flaked almonds
20 g (¾ oz) icing sugar

Cream
40 g (1½ oz) butter, softened
20 g (¾ oz) praline paste or powder
125 g (4½ oz) crème patissière (see
Saint Honoré recipe on page 68)

Follow the basic macaroon recipe on pages 8–11, colouring the mix light brown. Stick a sheet of greaseproof paper to a baking tray with four small dabs of macaroon mix at each corner. Cut a cardboard circle 15 cm (6 inches) in diameter and use as a template to draw two circles on to the paper. Pipe the macaroon mix carefully around these to get two regular crowns. Leave to dry at room temperature for 30 minutes.

Preheat the oven to 145°C (fan oven 125°C), Gas Mark 1½.

Mix the butter and the praline paste or powder with the warm crème patissière. Put in the fridge.

Sprinkle the macaroon crowns with the flaked almonds then cook for 15 minutes. Immediately on taking them out of the oven, slide the greaseproof paper and crowns on to a moistened worktop.

Slide the crowns from the paper and put the least attractive on a serving plate. Fill a piping bag with the cooled cream and fill the first crown generously.

Finish the Paris-Brest with the second crown, pressed lightly on top, and lightly dust with icing sugar.

Pear, crème Chiboust and caramel macaroons

Preparation time: 40 minutes
+ 1 hour drying
Cooking time: 15 minutes
Makes around 20 macaroons of
8 cm (3¼ inches) diameter

You will need 20 stainless steel
circles, 8 cm (3¼ inches) in
diameter, or 20 disposable
aluminium trays of the same
diameter

For the macaroon mix, see recipe
on pages 8–11
caramel food colouring
200 g (7 oz) caster sugar
8 pears, peeled, cored and diced
20 g (¾ oz) pectin
brown sugar

Crème Chiboust*
500 ml (18 fl oz) milk
1 vanilla pod
6 egg yolks
70 g (2½ oz) caster sugar
25 g (1 oz) plain flour
25 g (1 oz) cornflour
50 g (1¾ oz) butter, softened
25 g (1 oz) pectin

Italian meringue
80 ml (2¾ fl oz) water
175 g (6 oz) caster sugar
7 egg whites

Follow the basic macaroon recipe
on pages 8–11 and colour it
caramel. Prepare macaroons of 8 cm
(3¼ inches) diameter. Leave to dry for
an hour. Preheat the oven to 145°C
(fan oven 125°C), Gas Mark 1½.
Cook for 15 minutes.

Make the cream: heat the milk over
a low heat with the vanilla pod split
in two. In a bowl, beat the egg yolks
and the sugar, then add the flour and
the cornflour and beat again. Remove
the vanilla pod, pour the warm milk
over the mixture and return to the
heat, mixing constantly until thick.
Add the butter and the pectin and
mix. Leave the cream in the saucepan
without letting it cool.

In a different saucepan, bring the
water and the caster sugar to the
boil. Without mixing, make sure the
temperature of the syrup does not
exceed 120°C (250°F).

Meanwhile, whisk the egg whites
until stiff with a spoonful of sugar
syrup. Stop cooking the sugar once it
has reached 120°C (250°F) and slowly
pour over the beaten egg whites.
Continue to beat the meringue for
at least 5 minutes.

Incorporate a third of the beaten
meringue into the cream, which
should still be warm. Delicately add
the rest and mix with a spatula.

Pour the cream into the stainless
steel circles or tart trays so it is 1 cm
(½ inch) deep and put in the freezer.

Melt the caster sugar in a saucepan
until it is slightly caramelised then add
the pears. Stew for 5–6 minutes then
add the pectin. Keep in the fridge.

To assemble, spread out the macaroon
shells, fill with pear, then place the
cream discs on top. Sprinkle with
brown sugar and caramelise with
a blowtorch or under the grill.

***Note:** The crème Chiboust is a
slightly jellied pastry cream mixed
with Italian meringue while warm.

Chocolate and raspberry trifles

Preparation time: 30 minutes
Cooking time: 15 minutes +
  1 hour cooling
Makes 6–8 trifles

raspberry and rose macaroon shells

Raspberry jam
80 g (2¾ oz) caster sugar
50 ml (1¾ fl oz) water
300 g (10½ oz) raspberries
30 g (1 oz) pectin

Chocolate cream
100 ml (3½ fl oz) milk
150 ml (5 fl oz) single cream
3 egg yolks
30 g (1 oz) caster sugar
125 g (4½ oz) dark chocolate,
  broken into pieces

For the raspberry jam, dissolve the sugar in the water over a low heat then add the raspberries. Cook for no more than 2–3 minutes. Add the pectin, mix well and divide between glass serving pots. Put in the fridge.

For the chocolate cream, heat the milk and the cream in a saucepan over a low heat. Beat the egg yolks and the sugar together in a mixing bowl, pour over the boiling milk and cream, mix and return to a low heat to make a custard. Pour the cream over the broken chocolate and mix well. Leave to cool at room temperature.

To assemble the trifles, sprinkle broken macaroons over the raspberry jam, then add a layer of the chocolate cream.

Before serving, finish the trifles with pretty shells or pieces of macaroon, like a crumble.

Macaroon charlotte

Preparation time: 30 minutes
Serves 6–8

You will need 1 charlotte mould or a
deep Tupperware dish

around 50 purple, white and pink
macaroon shells
125 g (4½ oz) fresh raspberries

Raspberry mousse
4 sheets of gelatine
125 g (4½ oz) raspberry purée or
coulis
2 egg whites
75 g (2¾ oz) caster sugar
250 ml (9 fl oz) whipping cream

For the mousse, soften the gelatine
in cold water for 1 minute.

On a low heat, warm half the
raspberry purée or coulis. Remove
from the heat. Drain the excess
moisture from the gelatine then
dissolve in the warmed purée. Add
the rest of the purée and mix well.
Leave to cool at room temperature.

Beat the egg whites until stiff. Add
the sugar whilst beating until you get
a firm meringue. Whip the cream.

With a spatula, gently mix the cooled
purée into the whipped cream and
then mix into the meringue.

To assemble the charlotte, cover the
bottom and sides of the mould or
Tupperware with the prettiest
macaroon shells, in alternating
colours. Cover the lid of the mould or
Tupperware in the same way to
contain the mousse.

Pour in a layer of raspberry mousse,
then add a layer of macaroon shells.
Build up in successive layers,
finishing with a final layer of shells.
Refrigerate for at least 2 hours.

To turn out the charlotte, dip the
mould in warm water for a couple of
seconds. Turn out on to a serving
plate and decorate with fresh
raspberries.

Saint Honoré with macaroons

Preparation time: 40 minutes
Resting time: 30 minutes
Serves 7–8 people

1 roll of puff pastry
100 ml (3½ fl oz) water
250 g (9 oz) caster sugar
50 g (1¾ oz) glucose
red food colouring
around 15 pale red filled macaroons

Crème patissière
500 ml (18 fl oz) milk
½ vanilla pod
6 egg yolks
125 g (4½ oz) caster sugar
20 g (¾ oz) plain flour
20 g (¾ oz) cornflour

Whipped cream
½ vanilla pod
500 ml (18 fl oz) whipping cream
50 g (1¾ oz) icing sugar

The day before, make the crème patissière. Over a low heat, simmer the milk with the vanilla pod. Beat the egg yolks and the sugar together, then add the flour and the cornflour and beat again. Strain the hot milk into the mixture and return to a low heat, mixing continuously for 3–4 minutes until thick. Keep the cream in an airtight container in the fridge.

Unroll the pastry until nice and flat on the work surface.

Using a 24 cm (9½ inch) diameter cake tin as a template, cut the pastry into a regular circle. Put on a clean, dry baking tray and leave at room temperature for 30 minutes.

Preheat the oven to 200°C (fan oven 180°C), Gas Mark 6.

In a saucepan, boil the water, sugar, glucose and food colouring. Without stirring, make sure that the temperature of the syrup does not exceed 120°C (250°F).

Cover a baking tray with a sheet of greaseproof paper.

Stop the syrup cooking at 120°C (250°F) and leave for 2 minutes.

Meanwhile, cook the pastry for 7–8 minutes (if you see that the pastry is rising too much, cover with another baking tray).

Dip each macaroon into the syrup and arrange on a tray. Make sure the remaining syrup does not harden by warming slightly.

Put the cooked pastry on a serving plate and stick the macaroons on top with the remaining syrup. Leave to cool in a dry place at room temperature.

Beat the crème patissière to thicken and pour over the bottom of the Saint Honoré. Scrape the vanilla seeds into the cold cream, then whip. Add the icing sugar. Fill a piping bag and neatly cover the Saint Honoré.

Note: It is better to keep the Saint Honoré at room temperature and fill with the creams just before serving because cooked sugar does not keep well in too cold or humid an environment.

Macaroon pyramid

Preparation time: 30 minutes

You will need a polystyrene cone,
  30 cm (12 inches) high

75–80 macaroons filled with a thick
  ganache or cream

Royal icing
2 egg whites
juice of 1 lemon
500 g (1 lb 2 oz) icing sugar

Prepare the royal icing. In a mixing bowl, mix the egg whites, the lemon juice and the icing sugar until thick but still fairly loose. To relax the royal icing add a little egg white. To make firmer, add more sugar. You can even colour the icing if you like.

Assemble the pyramid. With a metal spatula, spread a thin even layer of royal icing on the polystyrene cone. Stick the macaroons on, starting at the base of the cone and alternating the colours.

Note: The royal icing glues the macaroons well. Once dry, it's like cement. You should not assemble the pyramid too long before serving. You can also stick the macaroons on to the cone with melted chocolate instead of royal icing.

Index

Conversion tables

The tables below are only approximate and are meant to be used as a guide only.

Approximate American/ European conversions

	USA	Metric	Imperial
brown sugar	1 cup	170 g	6 oz
butter	1 stick	115 g	4 oz
butter/ margarine/ lard	1 cup	225 g	8 oz
caster and granulated sugar	2 level tablespoons	30 g	1 oz
caster and granulated sugar	1 cup	225 g	8 oz
currants	1 cup	140 g	5 oz
flour	1 cup	140 g	5 oz
golden syrup	1 cup	350 g	12 oz
ground almonds	1 cup	115 g	4 oz
sultanas/ raisins	1 cup	200 g	7 oz

Approximate American/ European conversions

American	European
1 teaspoon	1 teaspoon/ 5 ml
½ fl oz	1 tablespoon/ ½ fl oz/ 15 ml
¼ cup	4 tablespoons/ 2 fl oz/ 50 ml
½ cup plus 2 tablespoons	¼ pint/ 5 fl oz/ 150 ml
1¼ cups	½ pint/ 10 fl oz/ 300 ml
1 pint/ 16 fl oz	1 pint/ 20 fl oz/ 600 ml
2½ pints (5 cups)	1.2 litres/ 2 pints
10 pints	4.5 litres/ 8 pints

Liquid measures

Imperial	ml	fl oz
1 teaspoon	5	
2 tablespoons	30	
4 tablespoons	60	
¼ pint/ 1 gill	150	5
⅓ pint	200	7
½ pint	300	10
¾ pint	425	15
1 pint	600	20
1¾ pints	1000 (1 litre)	35

Oven temperatures

American	Celsius	Fahrenheit	Gas Mark
Cool	130	250	½
Very slow	140	275	1
Slow	150	300	2
Moderate	160	320	3
Moderate	180	350	4
Moderately hot	190	375	5
Fairly hot	200	400	6
Hot	220	425	7
Very hot	230	450	8
Extremely hot	240	475	9

Other useful measurements

Measurement	Metric	Imperial
1 American cup	225 ml	8 fl oz
1 egg, size 3	50 ml	2 fl oz
1 egg white	30 ml	1 fl oz
1 rounded tablespoon flour	30 g	1 oz
1 rounded tablespoon cornflour	30 g	1 oz
1 rounded tablespoon caster sugar	30 g	1 oz
2 level teaspoons gelatine	10 g	¼ oz